D1409354

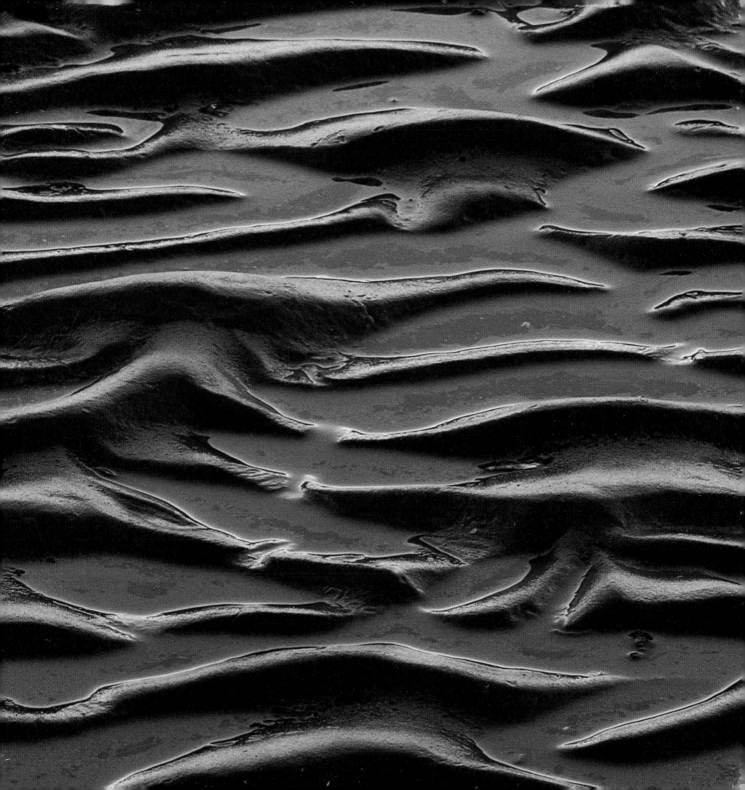

Published by Creative Education
123 South Broad Street, Mankato, Minnesota 56001
Creative Education is an imprint of The Creative Company

Art direction by Rita Marshall
Production design by The Design Lab

Library of Congress Cataloging-in-Publication Data

Hidalgo, Maria.
Color / by Maria Hidalgo.
p. cm. — (Let's investigate)
Summary: Explores the nature and many variations of color and its importance in our world.
ISBN 1-58341-228-X
1. Color—Juvenile literature. [1. Color.] I. Title. II. Series.
QC495.5 .H53   2002
535.6—dc21   2001047892

First edition

2 4 6 8 9 7 5 3 1

COLOR

MARIA HIDALGO

Creative Education

COLOR
MINING

Metals are found in many different colors. Bornite, also called peacock ore, can appear deep purple and blue, and turquoise has given its name to its own unique color.

Above, peacock ore
Right, a colorful garden
of tulips and daisies

What a boring world it would be if color didn't exist! Gray birds would soar through a gray sky, while gray people ate gray picnic food on a gray blanket in a gray park. The remarkable fact is that color, as most people think of it, does not exist. A bird, the sky, even grass does not have a color; rather, every surface absorbs some colors and reflects others.

COLOR
DISPLAY

Caused by intense solar activity exciting atoms in the upper atmosphere, the colorful aurora borealis can often be spotted on clear nights in northern parts of the world.

COLOR AND LIGHT

Light from the sun and other sources appears white. In reality, sunlight and lamplight, which both travel in waves, are made up of every color, all mixing together to create white light. Sir Isaac Newton, an English scientist working in the late 1600s and early 1700s, was one of the first scientists to investigate color. He used a **prism** to separate white light waves into a color spectrum and chose seven color names to identify the different wavelengths: red, orange, yellow, green, blue, indigo, and violet.

The sun's light contains every possible color

The materials in a compact disc reflect many colors, which is why rainbows seem to appear on its surface.

A prism works by bending each color wavelength to a slightly different **angle**. Made of glass or another transparent material, prisms are precisely cut with perfect edges, flat surfaces, and sharp corners. As each wave is bent, or refracted, the different colors emerge from the other side of the prism organized by wavelength. Red has the lowest frequency (the longest distance between waves), and violet has the highest frequency (the shortest distance between waves) in the visible light spectrum.

A prism refracting color wavelengths

COLOR

The highest arch of a rainbow (and the longest wavelength) is red; the lowest (and shortest wave-length) is violet.

8

Raindrops bend white light into seven-color rainbows

Rainbows occur the same way, except that raindrops, not prisms, refract the light. When the sun's white light enters a raindrop, it refracts into different wavelengths. These light waves then reflect off the back surface of the rain-drop, where they refract again as they pass out of the water. This reflection off the raindrop's back sends the light waves out at the same angle as millions of other rain-drops in the area, direct-ing them out in a circular pattern. The result is the curve in rainbows.

COLOR
VISIBILITY

The human eye sees warm colors before cool colors. Yellow is the most easily spotted, which is why it is used in clothing designed to increase visibility.

COLOR
FACT

If a human eye doesn't adapt from light to dark environments, or if it has trouble identifying images in dim light, it may suffer from a condition called night blindness.

The colored part of the human eye is called the iris

COLOR AND VISION

When light **illuminates** an object, some waves are absorbed and others are reflected. The human eye "catches" the light waves reflected off the object's surface and then activates the visual process. Light enters the human eye through the lens and stimulates the inside lining of the eyeball, called the retina. The retina is filled with color receptor cells called cones. Human eyes generally have three types of cones: those sensitive to blue, green, or red.

Working with other light-sensitive receptors called rods, the cones interpret the light waves into an image. Electro-chemical energy delivers the image from the retina to the brain. The retina is actually an extension of the brain. A lot of visual processing occurs within the eye before it even starts to travel through the optic nerve. According to some estimates, the human eye can distinguish 10 million different colors.

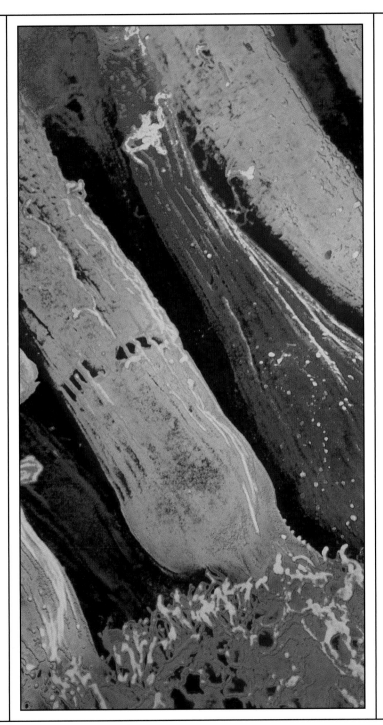

COLOR
BLINDNESS

A person is color blind if the cones in his or her retina do not sense blue, green, or red. In extreme cases, no color at all is perceived. This condition is called monochromatism.

COLOR
DEFINITION

As the eye ages, the lens turns yellow, affecting the eye's ability to tell the difference between some colors.

A few of the millions of rods and cones inside the human eye

12

The iris is an eye muscle that controls how much light enters the eye. The opening controlled by the iris is called the pupil. In bright light, the pupil is a tiny hole; in low light, the pupil dilates, or widens, to allow more light waves to enter the eye. The amount of **pigment** in the iris determines eye color. If very little pigment exists, the eye appears blue. As the pigment level increases, the iris and eye color become darker. All kittens are born with blue eyes, as are most human infants, because their dark pigments have not yet formed.

A cat with more pigment in one eye than the other

Color is very important to the survival of organisms, whether they are insects, animals, or humans. Colorful markings can serve as an **enticement** to the opposite sex during mating season. Color also identifies necessary objects (such as food or water) or potential dangers (such as a wasp's yellow and black stripes), and can camouflage, or hide, an animal or plant from predators or prey.

COLOR
FACT

Luminescence is the low-temperature light emitted by some animals and insects, such as jellyfish and fireflies.

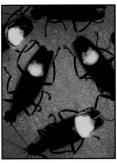

Above, fireflies
Left, a chameleon changing color

COLOR

VOCABULARY

The Inuit people of northern Canada and other northern parts of the world have 17 words for the English word "white." Each refers to a different type of snow.

An arctic fox camou-flaged by its white coat

Camouflage is one of nature's most effective protection devices, allowing plants and animals to blend into their surroundings. The white fur of an arctic hare helps the animal vanish in the snow. Bright vertical stripes disguise a tropical fish swimming through swaying seaweed. The chestnut and white feathers of a saw-whet owl disappear among the branches and bark of a shady forest. Many other animals, such as arctic foxes, hermit crabs, and three-toed sloths, also benefit from natural camouflage.

Sometimes an animal's coloring mimics other creatures and disguises the animal's true identity. For example, the American zone-tailed hawk looks similar to a small vulture. Vultures don't eat small rodents and reptiles, so potential hawk prey thinks it has nothing to fear when a "vulture" circles overhead. Using this disguise, the hawk has no trouble snagging unsuspecting prey.

15

Above, a blackbird Left, an iguana blending into the surrounding rock

The male of a species often has the most colorful and attention-getting markings. Male insects (such as fireflies), birds (such as peacocks), and apes (such as gorillas) all use a combination of color and courtship behavior to attract potential mates.

Octopuses, which are capable of changing **hues**, use their brilliant colors to warn intruders to stay away. Often, a dominant male octopus protecting his territory can win a battle without ever coming in physical contact with his opponent just by flashing different colors to signal his **aggression**.

COLOR
WAVES

The sky and the ocean appear blue because water molecules in the air and ocean scatter blue light waves easier than the waves of other colors.

COLOR
DEFENSE

Cephalopods, including octopuses and cuttlefish, change color to startle predators and to hide in ocean depths. They do this by changing the size of pigment cells in their skin.

***Left, an octopus
Far left, the vibrant
feathers of an adult
male peacock***

COLOR
RARITY

The color red is somewhat rare in nature, so it is often perceived as a sign of danger, possibly due to its association with blood.

Wasps can inflict painful stings when disturbed

The colors red, black, and yellow are often found on insects that have spines or are able to sting, ensuring that organisms with these colors are avoided by predators whenever possible. Copy-cat insects, those with similar color-ings, have evolved, and while they do not have the same spiny or stinging defenses, the colors of these insects can be enough to scare away most threats.

COLOR AND PLANTS

Many plants depend on insects and other organisms for pollination as well as to spread their seeds for the next season. Flower color and shape help bees, butterflies, bats, and birds identify sources of food and pollen. But flowers are often more colorful than we can see. Many flowers reflect ultraviolet light as well, which is invisible to the human eye but visible to most insects. In fact, many plants have flowers that are barely visible to us, but when photographed with an ultraviolet camera, they appear to be in full bloom. The darker color patterns often found in a flower's center guide bees to the nectar and, at the same time, to the pollen necessary for creating new seeds.

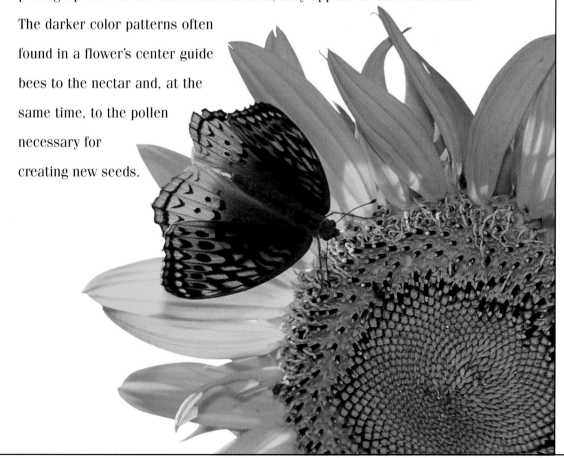

A butterfly pollinating a sunflower

COLOR
ADAPTATION

Birds that catch insects in midair depend on sharp vision and helpful colorization, such as black bills, which don't reflect sunlight into the birds' eyes.

COLOR

GARDENING

Hydrangeas have blooms that change color depending on soil nutrients. Acidic soil causes blue flowers; alkaline soil causes pink blooms.

Above, colorful hydrangea blooms Right, plants convert air, light, and water into food

All plants contain a pigment called chlorophyll. This chemical enables leaves to use the energy found in light waves, carbon dioxide in the air, and water from the ground to create food in the form of sugars called carbohydrates. Oxygen is also created and released back into the air. The entire food-making process is called photosynthesis.

Chlorophyll also gives plants and trees their green color, reflecting green light waves while it absorbs blue and orange light. In the autumn, as sunlight hours grow shorter, trees make less chlorophyll, making other pigments, which reflect the yellow and orange light wavelengths, more visible.

Reduced chlorophyll levels make leaves turn color

COLOR
HISTORY

In 30,000 B.C., Stone-Age painters made the earliest known use of color, grinding earth, stones, and plants into red, yellow, and black pigments.

COLOR
TERMS

The saturation of a color is called its intensity. If a color has been mixed with gray or white, it is less saturated and more muted, or toned down.

A colorful painting by Salvadorian artist Isaias Mata

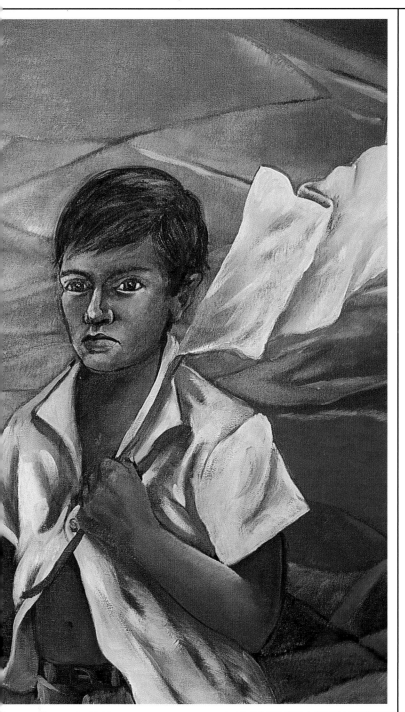

Artists organize colors in a similar fashion to the rainbow, but instead of placing colors in adjoining stripes, artists organize them in a circular color wheel. Red, blue, and yellow are called the three primary colors. They form the basis of a color wheel. All other colors can be created from these three; no other colors can create them.

COLOR
MOOD

Colors can be used to change the feeling in a room: painted white, a room seems larger and more spacious; a darker color creates a warm, cozy feeling.

COLOR
FACT

Before explorers brought oranges to Europe from the Middle East, there was no name for that color.

23

COLOR
TRICK

*When a person stares at a pattern of colors for a long time and then looks at a white area, a **negative** afterimage appears in complementary colors.*

COLOR
NEIGHBORS

The way colors look can be affected by the colors around them. Any color seems lighter when placed next to a darker color, and vice versa.

Orange and green are secondary colors on the color wheel

Secondary colors are created when two primary colors are mixed together. Red and blue make purple, yellow and blue make green, and red and yellow make orange. Mix a primary color with a secondary color, and an intermediate color appears, also known as a tertiary color: red-orange, indigo (a mixture of blue and purple), yellow-green, and so on.

Colors that are directly next to each other on the color wheel are called analogous colors. Complementary colors are those that are exactly opposite each other on the color wheel and, as the name suggests, enhance and balance each other well. When complementary colors are placed next to each other, they seem more vibrant and bright than when they are alone.

COLOR
CHANGE

Some elements change color when held in a flame because heat adds energy to a material's atoms, which then release their own energy in a different-colored light.

Lemons seem brighter next to darker-colored blueberries

COLOR
MOVIES

COLOR AND FILM

Photography captures light waves to create a printed image. Derived from the Greek words *photos*, which means "light," and *graphein*, which means "to draw," photography was originally able to capture only black-and-white images. Auguste and Louis Lumière invented the first practical color photography in France in 1907. They used dyed starch on a glass plate to create a color filter, which allowed them to create full-color prints of their photographs.

Modern color photography works in a manner similar to the human eye. Light waves enter through a lens and land on a surface sensitive to color and light intensity, only, rather than the rods and cones of the human eye, the light waves are exposed to strips of film.

The Lumière brothers at work in their laboratory in Lyon, France

Chameleons change color based on air temperature, emotions (such as fright or anger), or a battle win or loss against another chameleon—but not as camouflage.

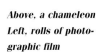

The two main parts of photographic film are a transparent, flexible base and a light-sensitive coating that captures light waves for a brief moment. The coating is made by taking silver and dissolving it in acid to create tiny crystals. Once the silver crystals are painted onto the strips of film base, the coating is capable of physically changing to represent the image. Finally, the film is developed, meaning it is treated to make the image permanent and then used to print the image on paper.

Above, a chameleon Left, rolls of photographic film

COLOR
TRADE

Humans have traded clothing dyes, paint pigments, and other sources of color since the beginning of recorded history.

COLOR AND SCIENCE

People respond to different colors in different ways. Color is often symbolic. Societies choose special hues to decorate or dress individuals to symbolize their importance or affiliation with a particular group or profession. However, between different societies and even throughout the world, certain colors seem to trigger similar reactions.

Red, orange, yellow, and brown hues are called "warm" colors and often have **associations** of cheerfulness, stimulation, and aggression. "Cool" blue, green, and gray colors make people feel secure, calm, and soothed.

To many Americans, the bold colors of their flag represent strength and freedom

COLOR
MOOD

Stage lighting uses color to create a certain mood or look. Colored glass or gelatin sheets stop unwanted colors, allowing only one wavelength to illuminate the stage.

A guard's bright-red coat warns intruders to stay away

COLOR
MEDICINE

Chinese, Indian, and Tibetan native healers have all used chromotherapy, the practice of using color to balance a body's energy.

Orange is one of the last colors given a name by a developing culture

Some colors have been proven to stimulate senses other than vision. For instance, red has been proven to affect the pituitary gland, which releases epinephrine. This causes rapid breathing, increased blood pressure, and the flow of **adrenaline**. Research has also shown that orange stimulates the appetite by affecting the body's nervous system. Blue triggers the brain to send out chemicals that relax the body.

The basic science of color is understood, but many aspects are still beyond explanation. For example, why do some cultures choose black to symbolize death, while others choose white? How does a person choose a "favorite" color? Why do certain colors seem to match while others don't? One thing is for sure: the scientists of tomorrow who choose to tackle these mysteries will lead very colorful lives.

COLOR PROPERTIES

Dark colors absorb all light wavelengths; white reflects them all. Wearing light-colored clothes on a hot day reflects light waves, keeping body temperatures cooler.

COLOR LANGUAGE

The first colors given names by the people of a developing culture are black and white. The next color is usually red, then yellow or green, followed by blue and brown.

Glossary

Adrenaline, also known as epinephrine, is a naturally occurring hormone that raises blood pressure.

An act of **aggression** is usually an unprovoked, forceful attack—a show of hostility.

An **angle** is created when two lines or planes intersect to form a corner.

Associations are links or connections to memories or emotions.

Something is an **enticement** if it lures or tempts.

Hues are different shades and gradations of colors.

Light **illuminates** an object when it lights it up, reflecting light waves into the eye.

Metabolic rates are the speeds at which different bodies use and create energy.

A **monochromatic** painting or drawing is created by using different shades of a single color.

An image's **negative** is its opposite; for example, dark areas on an image appear light on its negative, light areas appear dark.

A **pigment** adds color to an object, material, or plant or animal tissue.

A **prism** is a three-dimensional glass triangle, cut at precise angles to separate and bend different color waves.

Index

Photographs by Affordable Photo Stock (Francis & Donna Caldwell), Corbis (Bettmann Archive, Philip James Corwin), Dennis Frates, The Image Finders (Rob Curtis, Bruce Leighty, Carl A. Stimac, Mark & Sue Werner), KAC Productions (Bill Draker), Tom Pantages, Photo Researchers (Oscar Burriel/Science Photo Library, Omikron), Photri-Microstock (Bill Howe), Bonnie Sue Rauch, Tom Stack & Associates (Dave B. Fleetham, Robert Fried, J. Lotter Gurling, Kitchin & Hurst, Milton Rand, Inga Spence, Mark Allen Stack), Unicorn (Bob Coury, Russell R. Grundke, Paula J. Harrington, Andre Jenny, Novastock), Visuals Unlimited (Jeff J. Daly)